Zoefia Alexandria

ZOEFIA ALEXANDRIA
LoVE
ZoeY
FOUNDATION

Miracles
Can
Happen

ISBN:
978-1-63308-617-3 (paperback)
978-1-63308-618-0 (ebook)

Cover and Interior Design by *R'tor John D. Maghuyop*
Cover Photographs by *Michael Corrado*

CHALFANT ECKERT
PUBLISHING

1028 S Bishop Avenue, Dept. 178
Rolla, MO 65401

Printed in United States of America

Miracles Can Happen

Zoefia Alexandria

Thank You

We would like to give a heartfelt thank you to each and every person
that had an impact on our lives.

We thank her pastor, Bishop A.G. Blackwood, whom she loved dearly
and who prayed tirelessly for her recovery.

A special thank you to my beautiful daughter, Zoefia Alexandria who was always
so bright, selfless and so loving. You are my blessing, my best friend and my everything.
You will always be in my heart and your memory will forever live on.
I hope your story brings inspiration to others.

Xoxo Momma - Saphrona

Miracles can happen
In many different ways
Miracles can happen
On even the worst of your days

Miracles can happen
In any shape and size
Miracles can happen
Through a child's eyes

Every miracle has
A story deserving of being told
This is the story of Zoefia
A miraculous six-year-old

It was one morning
Something wouldn't give
Zoefia couldn't stand
And was given only four days to live

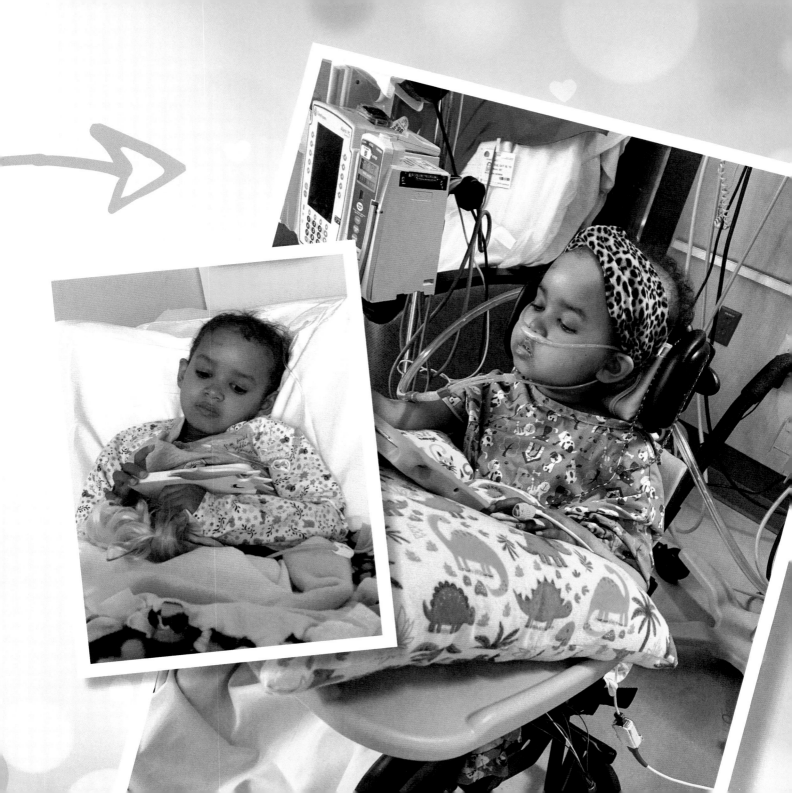

Put on life support,
In a coma for two months, subdued
But Zoefia would keep fighting
She would push through

Zoefia woke up
And never looked back
This miracle child worked hard
To get back on track

She forced herself to move again, and
Taught herself to talk
Zoefia fought hard everyday
And forced her legs to walk

Throughout all she had been through
Zoefia never lost her faith
She leapt over every hurdle
Along her grueling race

Zoefia is a miracle child
Who never gave up
She always showed she was tougher
When things got tough

Miracles can happen
But they take faith and love
When miracles do happen
Look for Zoefia in the sky above

100% of the proceeds of this book will be donated to the following charities:

Zoefia Alexandria Foundation
https://www.zoefiaalexandriafoundation.org/

Books That Heal
https://www.booksthatheal.org

Made in the USA
Middletown, DE
10 October 2020